# FACES OF THE OTHER

A CONTRIBUTION BY THE GROUP
**THINKING TOGETHER**

INTERRELIGIOUS RELATIONS AND DIALOGUE
WORLD COUNCIL OF CHURCHES

WORLD COUNCIL OF CHURCHES

# FACES OF THE OTHER

Produced by "Thinking Together"

Editor:
Hans Ucko

Editorial Assistance:
Yvette Milosevic

Photos, Design and Layout:
Barbara Robra

Published by:
World Council of Churches,
Interreligious Relations and Dialogue
150 route de Ferney
P.O. Box 2100
CH-211 Geneva 2
Switzerland
www.wcc-coe.org

Printed in Switzerland

ISBN 2-8254-1464-6

# TABLE OF CONTENT

# CREATING SPACE FOR THE OTHER

## IN OUR RELIGIOUS TRADITIONS

A man was lost in a dense, dark forest. As the daylight faded into the lengthening shadows of dusk and the thickness of night gathered, he became more and more frightened. After three days and nights of this painful feeling of being hopelessly lost, he became desperate.

Finally, on the fourth day of wandering about, at dusk, he saw a monster approaching him from afar. He filled his pockets with rocks to throw and prepared a heavy club from a branch with which to defend himself. His heart beat wildly in his breast. The perspiration of fear gathered on his brow as the monster loomed larger and larger as it approached. It was as tall as a man. He crouched behind some bushes. He grabbed for some of the sharpest stones and prepared to attack. As the monster came closer and closer he was frozen with fear.

Then, he realized that the horrible monster was a human being. He threw the stones away, but kept his grip on the club just in case. When the man was all but upon him, he threw the club away too as he threw his arms about the shoulders of the man. It was his own brother!

We easily see monsters, when we see each other at a distance. Our first reaction is fear, our second caution. Only when we are very close may we recognise the other as my brother or my sister. But it does not come easy. We have difficulties recognising other human beings as our brothers and sisters. They are other, they are not like us. They are different. It is easier to depict them as monsters and even to dehumanise them so as to best serve the stereotypes we have conveniently moulded, making it easier to avoid committing ourselves to working with and in our neighbourhoods to rescue that which is human and sacred in all the people about us.

Our time needs new ways to uncover human dignity and sanctity. Given the precariousness of peace in the world, we cannot go it alone any more, doing our own thing, ignorant of what the other is doing because he or she is too far way. We need each other. The world tells us so. We need a new discovery of each other, where not only the tribe, the clan, your own folk matters but the one you do not know. The one, who is the other. It is true that charity begins at home and that you cannot embrace everyone. In our need to discover the other, I am not talking about any universal love reaching out to all and everyone as the panacea. It may sound appealing but does not really touch the other. As it flies over the world it does not see the other. What is needed in the first place is not necessarily love but respect for the other and the realisation that we need each other. The search

7

for justice, peace, a sustainable environment and concern for human dignity cannot be undertaken by anyone of us in isolation. We are lost when we are alone. Is it when we are alone that we see the other as the approaching monster?

We are lost in a dense forest and unless we are willing to unlearn and learn anew, we will never get out of the forest. There are so many stereotypes, which we resort to in interpreting the presence of the other. It is easy to construct monsters, if we do not see the other as he or she is. Can we muster the faith and courage and strength, the capacity to care enough so as to throw away rocks and clubs and to embrace one another as sisters and brothers? Can we go about our labour of repairing our world together so that we can be a civilization worthy of God's love and care?

The story about the man lost in a forest fearing an approaching monster and in the end discovering that the monster was his brother ends in the following way. The man held on to his brother with love and gratitude. "Thank God you came in search of me. Please show me the way out of the forest, please."

One brother looked at the other with tears in his eyes as he answered: "I am lost now too, my brother. But I can show you what paths NOT TO TAKE. Together, we will find the way out."

The men and women, who have contributed to this booklet are part of a multireligious think-tank called "Thinking Together". Called by the World Council of Churches, this group of people of different faiths, with substantial experience of interreligious dialogue, are open to focusing together on some of the basic issues of belief and religion. Committed to our own religious tradition, we want to probe how we can explore common concerns together. One stirring question has emerged as a consequence of our exposure to the interreligious exchange of ideas and realities: How can we, in the midst of our religious diversity, express common convictions and explore core issues present

8

in all our religious traditions? As people committed to our different faiths, we are aware that we live in a world, which today deeply challenges our faiths in different ways. Religious plurality is one such challenge. How do our commitments as people of faith translate in our encounters with each other?

The group Thinking Together worked for some time on the whole concept of the other and realised that the very word has an ambiguous ring about it. Who is the other? And who says who is an other? The very notion "the other" is in itself something problematic. The other is not in him/herself an "other." The other is a construction. Others make the other. Someone says that I am an "other" but I am not an "other." The "other" is created. Creating otherness opens up for the possibility of marginalisation, denigration and exclusion. Isn't one of the elements of the violence in our world that of "other making"? And our religious traditions have contributed to making particular groups into "others". Xenophobia is familiar in the world of religion.

Throughout our conversations with each other in the group, in our thinking together, we wrestled with questions in relation to the other. These questions might be useful in discussions where people, either in their own communities or in interfaith meetings, want to reflect on the topic of the other.

**1. Does the other in his or her otherness challenge my faith or religion? Does my religious tradition provide space for the integrity of the other in his or her otherness?**
**2. Against whom, or in relation to whom, has our tradition defined itself? Who is the**

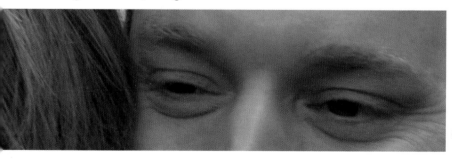

"other" (foreign, dangerous, etc.) against whom or in relation to whom our tradition defined itself at various times in our history? How was the "other" represented and why was the other represented in this way?

3. Has the perception of the "other" remained constant or has there been a change throughout history? Is there a new "other" against whom we define ourselves today? Who is it casting as the "other" now, and by what means?

4. Images of the other are often related to images of God. How is our understanding of faith influenced by the proximity to the other?

5. How can we contribute towards making the marginal other a significant other? How can we overcome the other being conceived as negative?

In this booklet a story is told from each of our religious traditions, reflecting how our religious traditions have wrestled with how to look upon the other. A story is told from our holy scriptures or from an oral tradition on how each of our religions tries to go from xenophobia, fear of the stranger to philoxenia, love of and respect for the stranger or "the friend of strangers."

The same law shall apply to the native as to the stranger who sojourns among you. (Ex. 12,49)

Do not neglect to show hospitality to strangers, for by doing that some have entertained angels without knowing it. (Hebr.13, 2)

O people, we created you from the same male and female, and rendered you distinct peoples

and tribes, that you may recognize one another. The best among you in the sight of GOD is the most righteous. GOD is Omniscient, Cognizant. (Qur'an, 49:13)

May all beings be happy and secure; may their minds be contented. Whatever living beings there may be - feeble or strong, long (or tall), stout, or medium, short, small, or large, seen or unseen, those dwelling far or near, those who are born and those who are yet to be born - may all beings, without exception, be happy minded! Let not one deceive another nor despise any person whatever in any place. In anger or ill will let not one wish any harm to another. Just as a mother would protect her only child even at the risk of her own life, even so let one cultivate a boundless heart towards all beings. Let one's thoughts of boundless love pervade the whole world - above, below and across - without any obstruction, without any hatred, without any enmity. (Metta Sutta, SuttanipÐta, vv. 145-150)

One who sees the supreme Lord, Existing alike in all beings, Not perishing when they perish, Truly sees. (Bhaqgavadgita 13:27)

The following stories witness to something interesting. Common for all of the stories, whether they come from our holy scriptures or from our oral traditions, a change of mind is taking place. The texts go from "othering" to creating space for the other as a significant other. The stories break the boundaries, make people discover something beyond and challenge people to reckon with something different.

It is our hope that these stories will contribute to a new reading of those dimensions in our religious traditions that help us provide or create space for the other as a significant other. It is only in this way that we as religious persons shoulder our responsibility to contribute to another reading of plurality, not as a threat, a monster that one needs to defend oneself against but the other as a brother or sister, a possible partner in making our society and world liveable.

[1] The story was first told by the late Rabbi Marshall Meyer at the WCC Assembly in Canberra 1991. I have shortened it and modified it a bit to suit the purpose of this booklet.

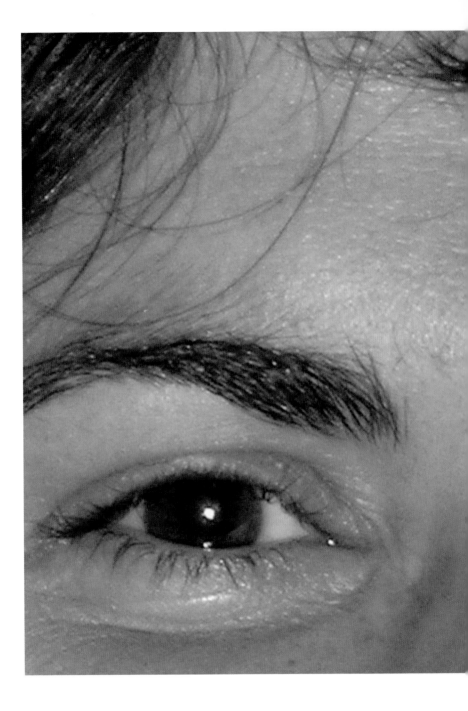

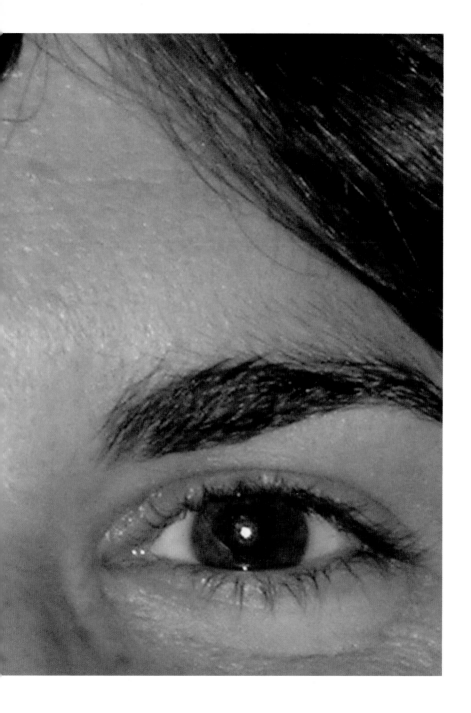

# INCLUDING WOMEN

## IN THE SANGHA

For Buddhists, the community (sangha in the original Buddhist languages) is one of three main refuges or shelters that help people cope with their life situation and bring them solace, comfort, and companionship. For Buddhists, the community can mean several things. It can mean the whole community, but it has meant especially the monastic community, consisting of monks and nuns. Buddhist monastics leave behind conventional family and professional lives to devote themselves wholeheartedly to a life of study, meditation, and service. Though relatively few Western Buddhists become monks or nuns, monasticism has always been central to Asian Buddhisms and monks and nuns have been highly honored and revered.

Nevertheless, the Buddha did not initially include women in his monastic sangha. The Buddhist religion stems from the Enlightenment experience of the historical Buddha, who lived in the sixth century before the rise of Christianity. At the time of his Enlightenment, the Buddha was already living a monastic lifestyle, which was common in his day and age. It is not surprising, given the norms of his culture that very few women were among these homeless, wandering religious seekers. When the Buddha began to teach about what he had discovered during his Enlightenment experience, he taught those he readily encountered on the road - other male ascetics seeking deep spiritual insight.

But the Buddha also taught laypeople his Dharma, his message of liberation through deep insight into the nature of reality. Early lay converts to

14

the Buddha's message included many women. Thus, it is not surprising that eventually his women lay disciples sought for themselves the same monastic lifestyles that suited their fathers, brothers, sons, and former husbands so well. They could also point to the example of another famous teacher of the day, Mahavira, the founder of the Jain religion, which is still practiced in India. In his community, women were already becoming nuns and renouncing conventional life just as their men had done.

Some five years after the Buddha became enlightened and began to teach, Mahaprajapati, his aunt who was also his foster mother, visited him with a delegation of other laywomen. These women had traveled some distance to find the Buddha so they were weary and worn out when they arrived. They had come for one purpose. They wished to join the monastic sangha, as had so many of the men in their lives. But the Buddha asked them not to make such a request. Three times they asked, and three times they received the same request that they not ask for this privilege. The women left weeping, disheartened, but unbowed. At this point,

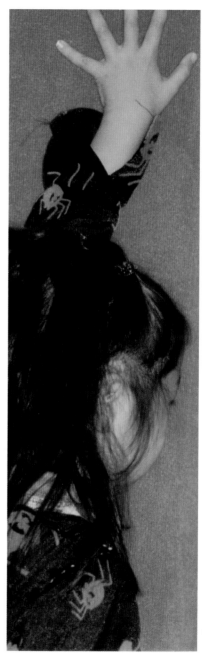

15

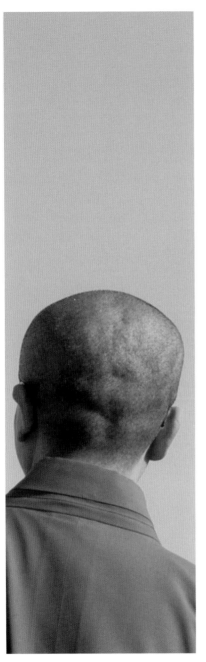

they resolved to pursue their request, and made the request more insistently by taking the initiative to cut off their own hair and put on saffron-colored robes, the visible marks of the Buddhist monastic sangha. They then traveled, by foot again, to the Buddha's next stopping point, arriving even more exhausted and beaten down by harsh traveling conditions than the first time.

This time, the Buddha's attendant Ananda, who was one of his favorite disciples, saw them first. He was deeply impressed both by their zeal and by their road-weary appearance and decided to plead their case with the Buddha himself. Three times he suggested to the Buddha that it would be a good idea if he granted the women's wish, and three times he was told to cease and desist. Ananda decided he needed a different strategy and asked the Buddha if women were not just as capable of living a monastic lifestyle and attaining enlightenment as were men. In the end the Buddha had to concede that there was no good reason to prohibit women from becoming monastics. They were as capable of living that lifestyle as were men, and would benefit from it in the same way as men had. The Buddha relented, changed his mind, and ordained the first women in his sangha. To this day many women in many different Buddhist cultures and communities have benefited from his change of heart.

However, the story does not end only on this happy note. As price for admission to the monastic sangha, the women were forced to agree to the Eight Special Rules, rules binding on nuns but not on monks that have the effect of subordinating every nun to any monk. For example, a nun, no matter how long she has been ordained, must rise in the presence of any monk, even if he had been ordained only a few hours earlier. At communal gatherings, all the nuns must sit behind even the child monks who are still playing games rather than paying attention to what is happening. (It must be remembered that in Asian cultures, age and seniority are considered very important, and elders are always given precedence.) In some parts of the Buddhist world, complete ordination for nuns was eventually lost, and in many cases, nuns were much less well-educated than monks and received much less economic support.

On the other hand, despite these limitations, the opportunity to become a nun always provided women with some alternative, some other option, in situations in which they had little self-determination and could not survive on their own without the support of their families. The early period of Indian Buddhism gave us what may be the only scripture in any major religion that was written by women. In the *Therigatha, The Songs of the Women Elders*, various nuns sing joyously of the freedom and release they have found - freedom both from abusive human relationships and from spiritual torment. Though the nuns' order declined in India and in South-east Asia, it flourished in China and Korea. Today there are more nuns than monks in both Taiwan and Korea. The nuns are young, well-educated, assertive, and confident that they can navigate their own futures almost completely free from control by monks. Today, re-establishing the nuns' order in those parts of the Buddhist world where it had been lost is a high priority for many. Recently, as the result of co-operation between Buddhist women and men from all parts of the Buddhist world, including

17

newly emerging Western Buddhism, the first nuns' ordination in over one thousand years was held in Sri Lanka, a place that once had flourishing nuns' communities.

What can we learn from these stories?

First, religious communities concerned about including the others who have been marginalized usually do not have to look outside their own boundaries. Religions frequently have created a cruel and incomprehensible internal division into insiders and outsiders. Discrimination between women and men is one of the most common of such internal divisions. Many religions do not even see this discrimination as a problem. They have taught that women are lesser human beings who have their own roles and duties to perform which make them unfit for the religion's most prized pursuits - prayer, study, reflection, meditation, scholarship, ritual leadership, becoming legal authorities or mystical leaders, among others. Religious leaders have no reason to praise themselves for their concern for the downtrodden and marginalized so long as they close off central religious pursuits to women in their own communities.

Second, there is no reason for despair over seemingly incomprehensible exclusion of others and hostility to these others. Things can always change, if only human beings decide to change them. Mahaprajapati did not take "no" for an answer, and neither have countless other women and men throughout Buddhist history who have looked at Buddhist practices that exclude or denigrate women and said, "These practices are fundamentally wrong, They are not in accord with Buddhist teachings, and they must be changed." Ananda got the Buddha to change his mind and in contemporary times the situation of Buddhist women, both nuns and laywomen, is improving dramatically in all parts of the Buddhist world because some people have made it their life's work to encourage such changes.

Finally, religious leaders can change their minds. The Buddha changed his mind about his former refusal to allow women to become nuns. Presented with determined people and irrefutable arguments, he simply changed his mind. That religious leaders can and should change their minds about conclusions made by themselves or their predecessors is the most important lesson to be learned from these stories. For far too often religious leaders simply repeat the mistakes of the past because they do not realize that it take far more strength and insight to retract a past mistake than to simply repeat it stubbornly. Steadfastness is admirable only when it is combined with flexibility and deep insight into what promotes peace and justice.

19

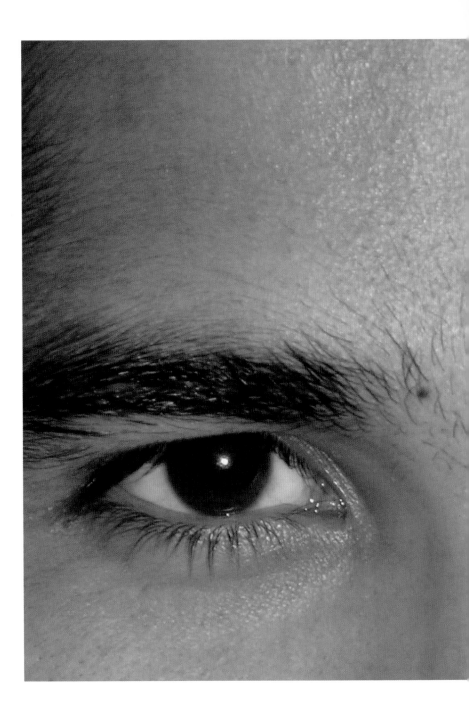

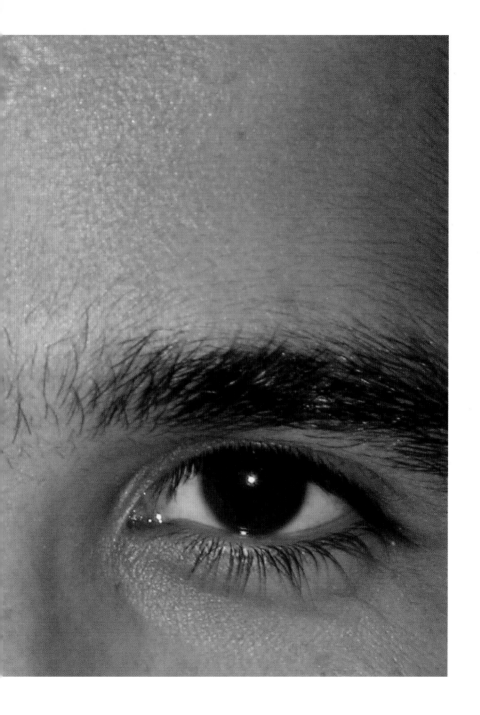

# Beyond Ambivalence: Peacemaking

## THROUGH THE PROPHETIC EXAMPLE

At this difficult time in Jewish-Muslim relations, many of us share a cry of anguish. Are Jews and Muslims condemned to perpetual conflict and hostility? Or are there possibilities within their common sacred stories for developing a theology of healing?

Our response is that hostility and enmity are constructed by human beings, and thus can be unmade by them as well. If we are to transform our relationship - for which there is dire need - the followers of Jewish and Islamic traditions must retrieve each other's humanity and end the mutual dehumanization that is currently taking place. One small but important step is to recognize that all of our sacred texts and stories provide opportunities for justifying violence as well as healing; all of our sacred texts and stories display "ambivalence." Arguing within the context of the Muslim sacred scripture, the Qur'an, Professor of Islamic Law Khalid Abou El-Fadl has provided a powerful response to this ambivalence. He contends: "The meaning of the text is often as moral as its reader. If the reader is intolerant, hateful, or oppressive, so will be the interpretation of the text."[1]

The way we talk about our sacred stories affects the way we think and ultimately the way we act. All of our sacred texts and stories provide possibilities for intolerant as well as tolerant interpretations. What is needed is a reinterpretation of the narrative, so that healing and a transformed relationship with the perceived enemy become integral parts of a renewed spiritual vision.

Yet this reinterpretation must be vital and transparently authentic. The movement toward reconciliation and the great-heartedness upon which it is based is complicated by fear: fear that the wellsprings of community resistance to injustice are under attack by insidious propaganda that seeks to "pacify" whatever is inconvenient. These fears are far from groundless - but we hold that they are irrelevant. For our study of our own tradition persuades us that generosity of spirit, which we find illustrated over and over in the life of the Prophet Muhammad (peace and blessings be upon him), is the only foundation upon which a truly just society can be built. And we believe the arguments for this are convincing.

Our first task is to acknowledge the fact of interpretive ambivalence, no matter how distressing that may be. Second we must muster faithful and coherent ways of dealing constructively with the texts, symbols, and rituals that display ambivalence. Third, and most importantly, we must base our arguments upon sacred stories that are unambiguously healing, lifting them up so that they stand out as beacons of hope and transformation.

We would like to offer two.

The second most sacred source of Islamic guidance after the Qur'an is the *hadith* literature, commonly called the Prophetic traditions. Imam Bukhari (d.870 CE) and Imam Muslim (d.865 CE) compiled two of the most widely respected and authoritative compendia of these traditions. These two works, named after their compilers, are sometimes referred to as the *sahihayn*, the "two most authentic" canons of *hadith*. They contain many overlapping reports. In one shared report, a companion of Muhammad, Jabir bin 'Abdullah, recalls the following incident:

**Once a funeral procession passed in front of us. The Prophet (peace be upon him) stood up; we stood up too. We said, "O Prophet of God! This is the funeral procession of a Jew!" He answered, "Whenever you see a funeral procession, you should stand up."[2]**

In a reinforcing report that immediately follows, two companions of Muhammad, Sahl bin Hunayf and Qays bin Sa`ad, recall that they were sitting in the city of Madinah when a funeral procession passed in front of them and they stood up. They were told that the funeral procession was of "one of the inhabitants of the land" - i.e., of a non-Muslim under the protection of Muslims. They relate:

**A funeral procession passed in front of the Prophet and he stood up. When he was told that it was the coffin of a Jew, he said, "Is it not a living being (soul)?[3]**

Interestingly some Muslims prefer to translate the latter part of this prophetic tradition as "Was he not a human being?"[4] While this may not accurately convey the literal words of the prophetic statement, it does represent the spirit behind it. However there is a profound implication in the literal words of the tradition. They remind Muslims that Jews too have souls that were breathed into them at birth by God. This interpretation resonates well with the primary source of Islamic guidance, the Glorious Qur'an. The Qur'an declares in verse 9 of Surah Al-Sajdah (Chapter 32) that:

This well-known Qur'anic injunction illuminates the egalitarian ethic contained in the prophetic tradition we have identified. This powerful ethic obliges Muslims to honor the dignity of all human beings, and to look upon each and every human being - whether he or she is a Jew, an atheist, or an adherent of an extra-scriptural religion - as carrying within her, within him, a part of God. This message is central to the Muslim view of humanity: every human life, Muslim or non-Muslim, has exactly the same intrinsic worth, because as the Qur'an teaches us, each one of us has the breath our God breathed into our being.

Our challenge is to work hard to reestablish this ancient core ethic as an integral part of contemporary Muslim culture and endeavor. Meeting this challenge demands that we transport the spiritual wealth of our sacred texts out of the realm of experts and into the

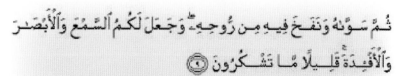

*[God] fashioned [the human being] in due proportion, and breathed into him something of His spirit. And He gave you [the faculties of] hearing and sight and feeling (and understanding): little thanks do you give!"*

public square. We need to demystify, "de-technicalize" religious communication - for while the apparatus of traditional scholarship has maintained the integrity of our received sources over many generations, it can also serve as a lock on the treasure-chest of truth. Too much reliance on experts disempowers the conscience of the person on the street, short-circuiting the basic Islamic claim of direct moral relations between the soul and God. So while the work before us calls for scholars; it also calls for popularizers.

26 Therefore the second *hadith* we would like to offer will be

told in a different mode, not as a citation but as an anecdote. (Scholars and the skeptical will want to know that it may be found in Sahih Bukhari, 8:626, other versions or fragments are at 3:594, 3:595; 4:610, 4:620, 6:162, 6:337, 8:524, 8:525, 9:52, 9:524, 9:564; narrators are Abu Hurayrah or Abu Sa`id al-Khudri.)

**It seems that in Madinah, a Muslim got into a dispute in the marketplace with a Jew. "Yes, by Him who made Moses the best of humanity!" swore the Jew.**

**The Muslim was incensed. "How can you say that?" he**

exclaimed, "when Muhammad is here among us?" And he hit him!

The Jew took his assailant before the Prophet. "Abul-Qasim," he said, "am I not protected here? And see what your follower has done!"

The Prophet became angry, which was as notable as it was rare. "How could you do such a thing?" he reproved the Muslim. "Don't you know that the prophets are all equal, and that none is less than any of the others? I would not make such a claim even about Jonah. As for Moses, when I rise on the Day of Judgment I will find him already awake, and I won't know whether he rose before me or whether he used up all his unconsciousness in his swoon on Sinai!" And he awarded damages to the Jew.

End of story: moral follows. First, although the Muslim in his impulsiveness acted at least partly out of love, he was still wrong. Respect for the other has priority: that is the sunnah of the Prophet. Second, the justice of Madinah was such that a Jew did not hesitate to complain against a Muslim before the leader of the Muslims, and won his case: that is the social achievement of the

Prophet. And third, the refusal to claim spiritual superiority demonstrated here: that *is in itself* the spiritual superiority of the Prophet.

If Moses had been there, would he have acted any differently?

"What is needed," we have claimed, "is a reinterpretation of the narrative, so that healing and a transformed relationship with the perceived enemy become integral parts of the renewed spiritual vision."

The problem lies in anchoring our reinterpretation of the narrative in such a way that it will convince, and endure. For if we merely assert that we must choose the peaceful textual interpretation over the violent one, then we are offering no principle upon which that choice is to be based, other than that we prefer things that way. The problem with this kind of argument is that the proponents of violent interpretations prefer things their way, too - and if private preference is the only key, why shouldn't they?

But private preference, in Islamic tradition, is always accountable to divine preference. God as self-revealed in the Qur'an expresses likes and dislikes in humanly comprehensible terms. Even though these terms themselves are susceptible to semantic nuancing based on the preliminary assumptions of each reader, the range of plausible readings is not infinite. Thus when the Qur'an declares that God loves the impartial or even-handed (*al-muqsitin*), it is not possible to read those words as proclaiming that God loves bias or self-interest. And when it declares that God does not love the corrupters of natural harmony (*al-mufsidin*), it is not possible to find there an authorization for its corruption.

"Proof-texting," the selection of particular passages to the exclusion of contradictory passages in order to justify one's views, is an affliction of all scriptural traditions. However, due to the very texture of the Qur'anic revelation and the Prophetic reports, it may be a greater temptation to readers of these scriptures than it is to others. What we can turn to for the control of arbitrary proof-texting is broader intimations of intent.

Thus 113 of the 114 surahs, or chapters, of the Qur'an begin

29

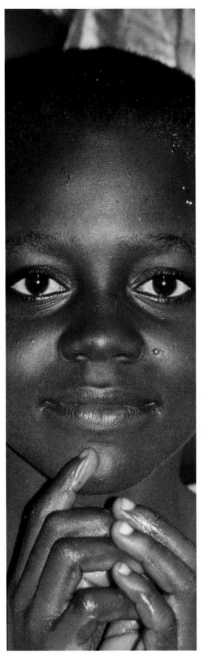

with the dedication *bismiLlah ir-rahman ir rahim*, which may be rendered "In the Name of God, the Compassionate, the Caring" or "In the Name of God the Benevolent, the Merciful," or in a number of other permutations of understanding centering always on the quality of selfless, wise, and tender love: *rahmah*. We have called upon *rahmah* earlier under the name of generosity of spirit.

*bismiLlah ir-rahman ir rahim* may *not* be read as dedicating the revelation, or our reading of it, in the name of the Vengeful, the Overpowering, the Punishing, the Excluding, or the Exacter of Retribution.

So 99.123% of the time, God's preferred perspective is stated, and it is not a perspective of wrath.

When we draw our conclusions as readers, do we consult with this preference of God? If not, where does our failure place us with regard to the divine will?

Again, in the matter of *hadith*, the reader may pick and choose. We are free to construct a Prophet "in our own image" by our selection among texts: he will certainly serve us as a mirror and show us our own needs. But can we ethically avoid the understanding of the Prophet proposed by God in the Qur'an? *Ma arsalnaka illa rahmatan lil-`alamin*: "We have not sent you except as *rahmah* to the worlds." We may not read this as meaning "as judgment over the worlds," nor either as *rahmah* to the Muslims alone. Rather the Messenger stands for compassion toward everyone and everything. That, if we are Muslims, is the direct statement of God about who Muhammad was, and what he was working for.

When we derive our principles from his acts, do we base them on the essence of his mission? If not, what does that failure tell us about how we are following him?

Anas bin Malik reported:

**The Messenger of God (peace be upon him) said to me: "My son, if you are in a position to pass your morning and evening keeping your heart free from malice against anyone, then act accordingly." He then said: "My son, *that is my sunnah*. Whoever loves my sunnah, in fact loves me, and whoever loves me will be with me in Paradise."**

The great scholar Imam Tirmidhi transmitted it (Hadith #175). We have added the italics ourselves. And God knows best.

[1] Khalid Abou El Fadl (2002), "The Place of Tolerance in Islam: On Reading the Qur'an-and misreading it."(*Boston Review*, 2/25/2002)
[2] *Sahih al-Bukhari*, Volume 2, Book 23, Hadith Number 398
[3] *Sahih al-Bukhari*, Volume 2, Book 23, Hadith Number 399:
[4] See for example; the Indian Muslim scholar, Mawlana Wahiduddin Khan, "The Spiritual Goal of Islam" See; http://www.alrisala.org/Articles/papers/goal.htm

31

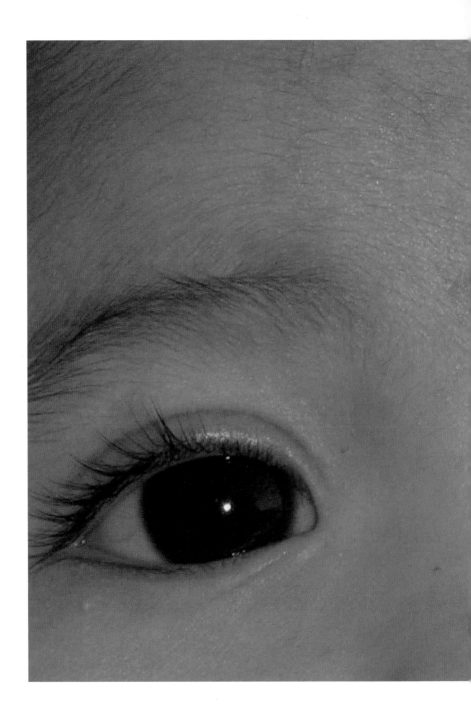

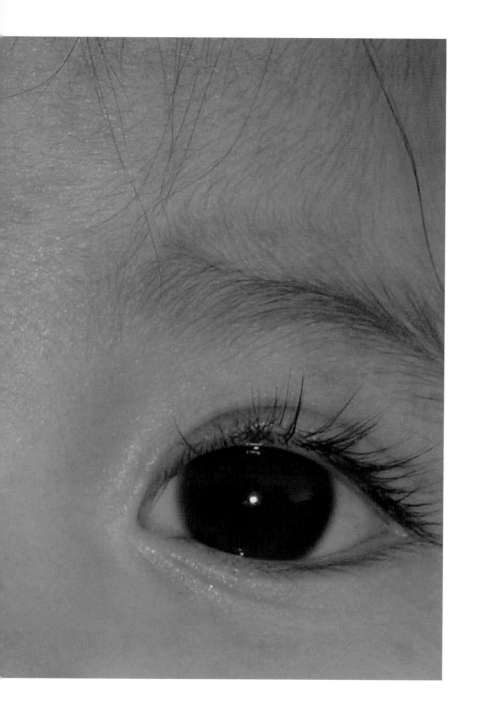

# Satyakama:
# The Boy
## Who Did Not Know
# His Father

The Chandogya Upanishad tells the story of a boy named Satyakama, who wanted to study the Vedas.[1] Satyakama was well aware of the caste requirements for such study and went to his mother.[2] "Mother," said Satyakama, " I want to become a Vedic student. So tell me what my lineage is."[3] Satyakama's question turned out to be a very difficult one for his young mother and we could only imagine her discomfort. "Son," she replied, "I don't know what your lineage is. I was young when I had you. I was a maid then and served and had a lot of relationships. As such, it is impossible for me to say what your lineage is. But my name is Jabala and your name is Satyakama. So you should simply say that you are Satyakama Jabala."

Encouraged by his mother's response, Satyakama went to a teacher named, Haridrumata Gautama, and expressed a desire to study the Vedas. "Sir," said Satyakama, "I want to live under you as a Vedic student. I come to you, Sir, as your student." Gautama responded with orthodox predictability. "Son, what is your lineage?" " Sir, I do not know what my lineage is," replied Satyakama. "When I asked my mother, she replied: 'I was young when I had you. I was a maid then and had a lot of relationships. As such, it is impossible for me to say what your lineage is. But my name is Jabala, and your name is Satyakama.' So I am Satyakama Jabala."

For Gautama, the question was routine, and so, perhaps, was every answer he had received before meeting Satyakama. He expected to hear the name of one of the ancient sages that would verify Satyakama's *brahmin* lineage. Knowing the rigidities of caste orthodoxy, a student, uncertain about his lineage, would not approach a Vedic teacher. If Satyakama's reply was unusual, so was the teacher's. "Who but a *brahmin* could speak like that!" answered Gautama. "Fetch some firewood, son. I will perform your initiation. You have not strayed from the truth."

Although Gautama asked the traditional question about Satyakama's lineage, Gautama's answer reveals his willingness to defy the prevailing custom. In a religious system that evaluated the value and potential of human beings by the circumstances of birth, Gautama responded to Satyakama as an individual and looked at the content of his character. Most teachers of the time, unable to establish Satyakama's biological lineage, would have turned him away because he was the illegitimate son of a maidservant who did not know his father's caste. He would be seen as unfit for learning because of inappropriate birth.

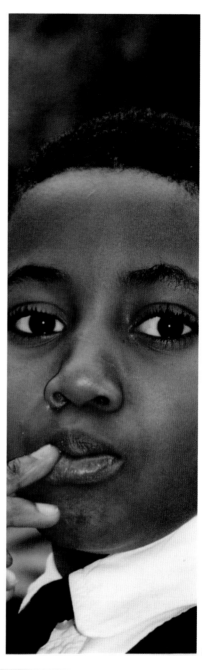

By telling the truth that he did not know his father, Satyakama put at risk the goal for which he had come to Gautama's door. There was a real possibility that he would be rejected and never have the opportunity to study the Vedas. For Gautama, however, it is this faithfulness to truth and not caste lineage that qualifies one for the study of the sacred texts. Being *brahmin* is defined, not by birth, but by fearless commitment to truth. Satyakama demonstrated this faithfulness through his willingness to speak the truth about a difficult and potentially embarrassing matter. His strong desire to study the scripture did not tempt him to compromise the truth.

It is quite possible that the encounter with Satyakama was a moment of awakening and transformation for the Vedic teacher. Before him stood a boy whose appealing eyes radiated an intense thirst for wisdom. Satyakama's physical presence along with his unabashed and transparent honesty, echoing the words of his mother, was challenging. How should he respond? Should he follow religious custom and inflexibly turn Satyakama away from his door without a response? Should he tell him that he is unfit to study the Vedas because he does not know who is his father? Or, should he defy custom and respond affirmatively to the real person before him whose love of truth was unquestionable? The challenge of Satyakama's presence and truthfulness enabled the teacher to discover the injustice and inadequacies of caste orthodoxy and to affirm that love of truth is more important than linage and circumstances of birth. It was a liberating moment for both teacher and student when the division between self and other was overcome.

---

[1] The four Vedas (Rg, Sama, Yajur and Atharva) are the authoritative scriptures of the Hindu tradition. The final section of each text is called the Upanishads and these take the form of dialogues between teachers and students. The Upanishads are over one hundred in number and believed to contain the highest wisdom of the Vedas.  The Chandogya Upanishad belongs to the Sama Veda and the encounter between Satyakama and

Gautama is to be found in Chapter 4.4.1-4.9.2. See *The Upanishads*, trans. Patrick Olivelle (Oxford: Oxford University Press, 1996).
[2] The caste system is a hierarchical social order consisting of four main groups. At the apex of the hierarchy are the *brahmins* (priests and teachers). Following the *brahmims* are the *kshatriyas* (warriors and political rulers), the *vaishyas* (merchants and farmers) and the *shudras* (laborers) who are expected to serve the first three groups. The system is rendered more complicated by its subdivision into thousands of sub-castes (*jatis*). Those who, for one reason or another, do not belong to one of the four castes are regarded as outcastes or untouchables and denied the rights and privileges accorded to the upper castes. The caste system has implications for religious practice. The first three castes are regarded as twice-born and are alone entitled to study the Vedas. It is a remarkably resilient system, even though changes are occurring as a consequence of legislation, democracy and urbanization.
[3] The actual term used by Satyakama for lineage is *gotra*. A *gotra* is a *brahmin* clan or group of families who trace their origin to a distant common ancestor. This ancestor is identified as an ancient sage. *Gotras* are transmitted through the male line. By inquiring about his *gotra*, Satyakama assumed, for some reason or other, that his father was *brahmin* and he belonged to the *brahmin* caste.

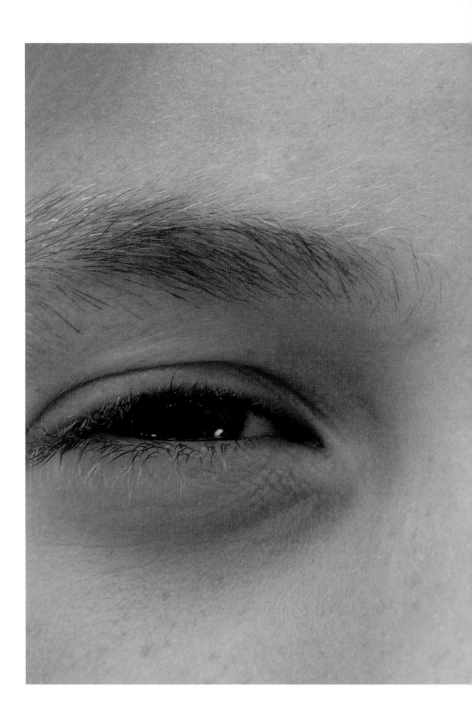

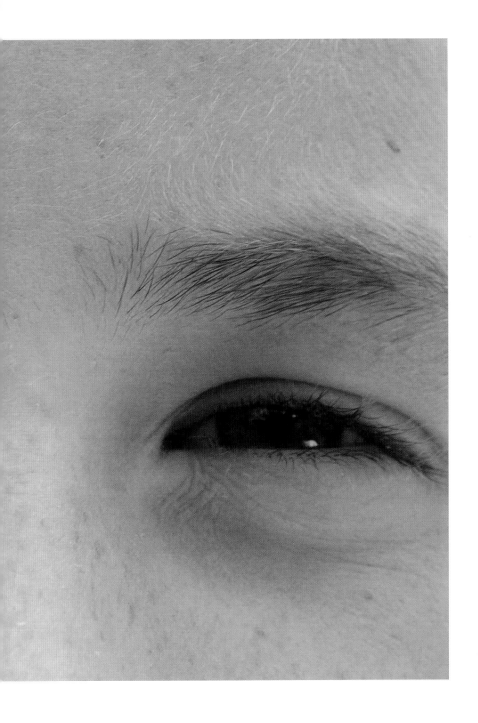

# AN ONGOING JOURNEY

Christians, throughout their history and in every part of the globe, have always worked strenuously at their religious identity. As a Christian from India, I am fascinated by the way Indian Christians have forged their religious identity. A dynamics of difference comes into play when an Indian Christian attempts to form his or her religious identity. This means that my Indian Christian identity is shaped by the way I formulate my being different from the Hindu "other" and the European "other." I am different from my Hindu neighbor, and I am also different from my fellow Christians in Europe who brought Christianity to my people. The Hindu-Christian difference, in particular, is often seen in a matrix of over-against-ness. Hindus are viewed as potential enemies and not as fellow-pilgrims on our journey towards the Divine. How does one move from a mode of being over against the Hindu to a posture of being alongside the Hindu? The story of Peter, a disciple of Jesus, has been an inspiration to many in this movement from over-against-ness to alongside-ness.

It was about noon, and Peter, while he was staying in Joppa at a friend's home, went up to the attic to pray[1]. It was time for lunch and he needed to wait for the lunch to be prepared. However, Peter was so tired and hungry that he fell into a trance. He had a vision in which a large sheet came down from the sky and "in it were all kinds of four-footed creatures and reptiles and birds of the air." That was indeed a surprise to Peter; yet more surprising was that "he heard a voice saying, 'Get up, Peter; kill and eat'." Peter said, "By no means, Lord; for I have never eaten anything that is profane or unclean." The voice said: "What God has made clean, you must not call profane." This happened three times and Peter woke up from his trance only to find that three soldiers had come to the door to invite him to an Army General's home in Caesarea. Their General, Cornelius, had seen an angel who instructed him to invite Peter and listen to him. There was no time for Peter to think through what this vision of blanket-full-of-creatures meant.

Peter did not know what to make of the invitation because it was from a Roman, one who is truly the "other" for Peter. He was reluctant to accept the invitation. However, there was an inner voice that whispered to Peter, "Now get up, go down, and go with them without hesitation." The next day, Peter, along with some of his friends from Joppa and the three soldiers, traveled to Caesarea. Even though it took a day for them to get to Caesarea, the journey was made enjoyable by long conversations. The soldiers told Peter how their

master was "an upright and God-fearing man," and how he was admired and "well-spoken of by the whole... nation." They also mentioned how Cornelius "gave alms generously to the people and prayed constantly to God." While listening to this description of this pious and devout man, Peter remembered what his fellow-disciple, James, used to say: "Religion that is pure and undefiled before God, the Father, is this: to care for orphans and widows in their distress, and to keep oneself unstained by the world."(James 1:27).

James's words "pure" and "undefiled" helped Peter to go back to the vision he had the previous day. The vision of the blanket was after all about seeing Cornelius, who is practicing a religion that is "pure and undefiled," in a new way. Cornelius is what one might call, "the other." He is of a different race, and belongs to a different religion. So in normal circumstances, Peter would consider him as being over against him and "unclean." Just like the way he would not eat unclean animals, he would not associate with those who were "unclean." But, Cornelius was a different kind of a man – a man who seemed to be practicing the pure and undefiled religion that James used to talk about. Moreover, did not Peter hear the voice say: "What God has made clean, you must not call profane?" Peter began to share with his group of fellow-travelers his feeling of confidence and conviction about visiting Cornelius and presenting the story of Jesus, the Christ to him.

One of the women from Joppa said to Peter, "I remember your telling us the story of Jesus and his interaction with a Canaanite woman. Is that not similar to what you are going through now?" "Yes, indeed," Peter said, "Jesus himself had to learn to see the other as alongside of him and not over against him." When a Canaanite woman came out and started shouting, "Have mercy on me, Lord, Son of David; my daughter is tormented by a demon," Jesus treated her as an "other" and said, "It is not fair to take the children's food and throw it to the dogs." She refused to be discouraged by those words, and said to Jesus, "Yes, Lord, yet even the dogs eat the crumbs that fall from their master's table." Jesus was truly amazed by her faith and courage and told her, "Woman, great is your faith! Let it be

43

done for you as you wish." As he narrated this story, Peter said, "Now I look back on that story and think of her faith and courage, I realize that the so-called other is no longer a stranger."

The conversation continued with Peter narrating more events from Jesus' life. He remembered the time when Jesus and his disciples passed through the Samaritan village of Sichar. It was noon time and they sat by the legendary well of Jacob. Peter and the other disciples had gone into the village to buy food. When they came back, they saw Jesus having a delightful conversation with a Samaritan woman, and they were truly astonished. None of them had the courage to ask Jesus, "Why are you speaking with a woman, and a Samaritan woman to that ?" Yet they knew that the Samaritan woman was not an "unclean" other for Jesus. One could clearly discover that by simply looking at the face of Jesus; and certainly the beaming face of the Samaritan woman and her radiant smile told the story of the unconditional acceptance she had received from Jesus.

This conversation with his fellow-travelers had convinced Peter that he was doing the right thing by going to Cornelius's house. Cornelius was no longer a stranger or an unclean other; he was truly a fellow-pilgrim in the journey of faith. Peter was quite convinced of it as they entered the house of Cornelius. Therefore when the conversation with Cornelius began, Peter said with a broad smile, "Cornelius, you yourself know that it is unlawful for me to associate with a person like you; but God has shown me that I should not call anyone profane or unclean. So when I was sent for, I came without objection. Tell me why you sent for me?" Cornelius narrated the vision he had and Peter was overjoyed.

When they all sat down to continue their conversation, Peter spoke with confidence, saying, "I truly understand God shows no partiality, but in every nation anyone who fears God and does what is right is acceptable to God." Peter knew he was right. He knew that he was saying something different from what he had told the people in Jerusalem months ago. At that time, he and John had announced healing to a lame man at the temple gate and the man was fully healed and was walking and praising God. People were amazed and asked, "By what power or by what name did you do this?" Peter attributed the healing to the name of Jesus of Nazareth and proclaimed, "There is salvation (or healing) in no one else, for there is no other name under heaven given among mortals by which we must be saved." Peter knew that he was in a new situation in Cornelius's house. He could not at this time make that type of sweeping claim for the name of Jesus. It was time to see the other as "acceptable to God." If so, his telling Cornelius the story of Jesus was simply one traveler's sharing of directions with another. Cornelius was deeply touched by the story of Jesus and asked to be included in the community of the disciples of Jesus.

Seeing the other as a fellow-pilgrim is not a one-time exercise; it has to be cultivated and sustained. Peter himself found it difficult to sustain such a vision. When some of the early converts complained about the inclusion of the people of other religious traditions, he wavered in his commitment to the new vision of the other. When Peter and other disciples together with Paul and Barnabas were in Antioch, Peter showed signs of returning to the pre-vision times. Paul writes about it this way: "Until certain people came from James, he (Peter) used to eat with others. But after they came, he drew back and kept himself separate." When Paul confronted Peter and corrected him, Peter was able to return to the vision that shaped his acceptance of the other (Galatians 2). Peter's story illustrates so powerfully the call to envision and develop a posture of acceptance toward the other, the stranger, and the "unclean." It also shows that our acceptance of the other is not always a smooth and consistent path; it often resembles a hesitant and jerky journey.

While this story is helping Indian Christians to see their Hindu neighbors as fellow-travelers, there is a shadowy side to this story as well. The shadowy side is not in the essential content of the story, but in the way this story is narrated. Neither Luke, the author of Acts of the Apostles, nor Peter was aware of this dark side. As an infant religious community, Christians found it necessary to place themselves over against their Jewish neighbors very similar to how Indian Christians placed themselves in relation to Hindus. While the story is

removing the over-against-ness in relation to Cornelius, it places the early Christians and Jewish people of those days in starkly oppositional terms. It paints the Jewish people as those who are over against Christians. It has taken a long time to bring to light this problematic view of the other and deal with it squarely. It took only a few years to admit Gentiles into the Christian church; but the church needed nearly twenty centuries to own up to its polemical and hostile relationship with the Jewish community. As a Christian in India, I find myself working through the story of Peter all over again to discover ways by which I and Christians all over the world may see our Jewish friends as fellow-pilgrims on our journey towards God.

It is abundantly clear that the movement from over-against-ness to alongside-ness is not a one-time event; neither is it dealing with only one group of religious other. It should be extended in time and space so that we recognize the shadow-side of our narratives, and discover new avenues of reconciliation with the other. Such reconciliation is a life-time process that needs to be maintained, cultivated, and nurtured. It calls for a community of mutual criticism. As Paul confronted Peter in his time, we Christians, Jews, Hindus, Buddhists, and Muslims need to challenge one another today, and thus move to an even more fully inclusive and living vision of beloved community.

---

[1] This particular story is found in the New Testament, in Acts of the Apostles, chapter 10. The quotes are taken from the New Revised Standard Version of the Bible.

47

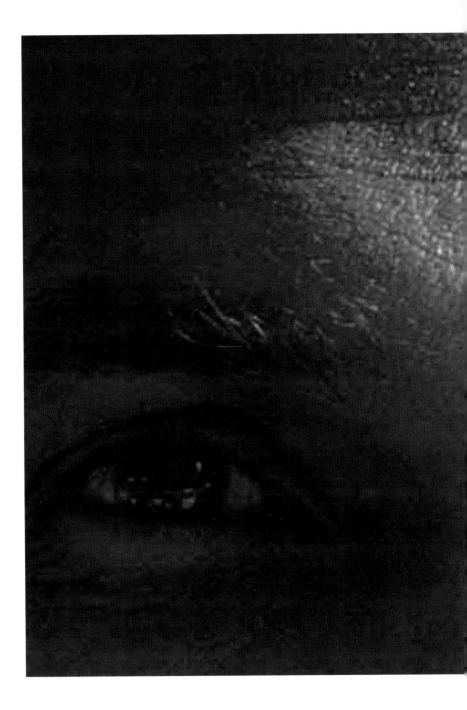

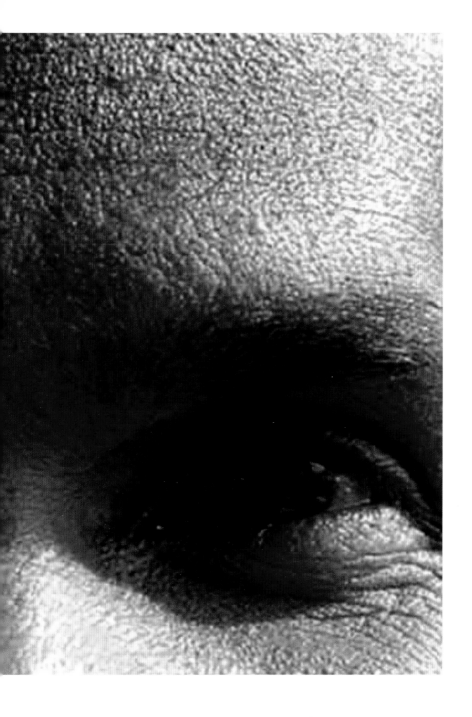

# FOR OURSELVES AND FOR OTHERS

The Hebrew word for responsibility, *achrayut, contains* within it two words: *ach,* which means "brother" and *acher,* which means "Other." The relationship of responsibility towards " brothers and others"[1] is one of the key issues in Judaism, both traditionally and in terms of modern Jewish life.

One of the prominent features of traditional Jewish religious life is the Dietary, or Kosher laws. In effect, these laws have limited the extent to which religiously observant Jews can mix with non-Jews in "companionship" (in the Latin, "cum panis" means, literally, "with bread;" companionship is "breaking bread together.")

Twice in the Torah - once in Leviticus 11: 13-19 and once in Deuteronomy 14:11-20

- we find a list of nonkosher birds. As distinguished from mammals and fish, these do not have general characteristics, such as cloven hooves or fins and scales. Rather, Biblical commentators have attempted to find meaning in the choice of particular species. One generally accepted category is that birds of prey are forbidden.

Among those listed is the *chassida,* the stork, not a bird of prey. It would appear that the name of this bird is derived from the word *chessed*, "lovingkindness." Our great medieval biblical commentator Rashi, following the earlier Rabbinic *Midrash,* asks, "Why is the bird called *chassida*? Because it performs acts of *chessed* by sharing its food with other storks." It took hundreds of years for the next logical question to be addressed; namely, then why isn't it Kosher? This question was asked in the 19th century by the Gerer Rebbe known as *Chiddushei HaRim*. The answer he gave: "Because it performs acts of *chessed* by sharing its food with other storks. Only with other storks."

In this short parable we have the potential strengths and weaknesses of religious communities; we have the dilemma of particularism and universalism. Strong particularistic communities do *chessed* towards members of their own group, but how do they relate to outsiders, who may be members of other communities? This is the educational challenge we have today: to develop proud young Jews, grounded in their own culture, who will not be like the storks, but like human beings who can show compassion and concern for members of other communities, as well.

One of the aspects of Jewish life which is often difficult for members of other faith-communities to grasp or relate to, is that Jews understand themselves as more than a religious community. They see themselves as members of an historic people, with deep

ethnic and cultural ties that go beyond religious belief and observance. Thus, even secular Jews may see their people as Chosen, even when they may have long ago rejected a belief in a Divine Chooser.

Clearly, an exhaustive study of the different approaches to the chosenness of the Jewish people is beyond the scope of a short paper. There have been many different approaches to this issue[2], ranging from a belief in the inherent superiority of Jews over other human beings, to a rejection of the concept as chauvinistic, irrational and inappropriate for a modern Jew (perhaps most notably in the work of Mordecai Kaplan, founder of the Reconstructionist movement[3].). The "Chosen People" has been called "the Choosing People." The interpretations

have included Election as a component of the Abrahamic Covenant, as the meaning of the Mosaic Revelation or as an embarrassment and affront to our moral sensibilities. Eliezer Berkovits wrote: "God did not choose the Jews, but the people that God chose became the Jewish people as a result of their taking upon themselves the task and responsibility for the realization of Judaism."[4] Jacob Agus, in a critique of such attempts to re-interpret the problematic concept, wrote:

*"It is not enough to resort to the usual homiletical devices—the Jews were chosen for service, not for lordship; they were given greater responsibilities; they were to consider themselves aristocrats of the spirit, endowed with the ardor of noblesse oblige; they were in the actual unfolding of their historic destiny the "Suffering Servant" of humanity.[5]*

Agus perceived those attempts as apologetic. In their stead, he suggested the following:

*"As a component of faith, the feeling of being 'covenanted' should be generalized; every person should find a vocation and dedicate himself to it. So, too, the pride of belonging to a historic people should be universalized. All men (sic! -DW) should take pride in the noble achievements of their respective peoples, scrutinize their national feelings, and guard against their collective weaknesses, even as we Jews are bidden to do."*[6]

His suggestion seems to draw from the idea, first found in the works of Samson Raphael Hirsch, that every nation was chosen for some purpose. Nevertheless, it is difficult to deny certain unique features of Jewish history and culture. Few other peoples share the historical and geographical breadth of Jewish existence. The complex amalgam of religion and nationhood, the Diaspora experience, the history of suffering and persecution, the modern renascence - all of these taken together seem to point to a special heritage. Still, following Agus, we might offer the possibility that other nations might be able to learn from the very dialectic of universalism and particularism with which Jews, especially in the modern era, have struggled—the question of brothers and others. As Agus summarized:" …we ought to be a chosen people, as example, not as exception."[7]

From the nineteenth century onward, with the advent of the European Enlightenment and Emancipation, many Jews have expressed their sense of

53

responsibility for brothers and others through involvement in various social movements, usually liberal, sometimes of a revolutionary or radical nature.[8] Many religious Jews turned inward and rejected modernity, because they feared its potentially negative effects on Jewish identity. One of the examples of a learned, traditional Jew who was involved in progressive social causes beyond the Jewish community was Professor Abraham Joshua Heschel (1907-1972.) Born in Poland to a renowned Chassidic family, he came to the United States in 1940 and five years later, became Professor of Jewish Ethics and Mysticism at the Jewish Theological Seminary, a post he held until his death. Poet-philosopher, social and political activist, prolific author, and, perhaps most of all, esteemed teacher, Heschel spoke out against the war in Vietnam and racial inequality in his adopted country. After marching with the Reverend Martin Luther King Jr. on one of the famous Freedom Marches, Heschel said: "I felt as though my legs were praying." At the same time, Heschel was an outspoken supporter of the State of Israel and the cause of Soviet Jewry.

In conclusion, Jews are challenged to be both particularists and universalists. A totally universalized human being is, in a sense, a dehumanized one. At the same time, an exclusively particularist approach is also potentially dangerous, feeding into ethnocentricity and even chauvinism or racism.

We can perhaps paraphrase the famous dictum of Hillel: "If we are not for ourselves, then who will be for us? But if we are for ourselves alone, what are we?"

---

[1] See an essay with that name by Sidra DeKoven Ezrachi in Reimer and Kates, (eds.) Beginning Anew: A Woman's Companion to the High Holy Days, New York: Simon & Schuster, 1997.

[2] See The Condition of Jewish Belief, a symposium compiled by the editors of Commentary Magazine, published in 1966 by the American Jewish Committee and MacMillan, New York, and Arnold Eisen, The Chosen People in America: A Study in Jewish Religious Ideology, Bloomington: Indiana University Press, 1983.

[3] Ibid., p.121.

[4] Ibid., p.26.

[5] Ibid., p.12.

[6] Ibid., p. 13.

[7] Ibid.

[8] See Paul Mendes-Flohr, The Jew in the Modern World: A Documentary History, Oxford: Oxford University Press, 1995.

# Thinking Together

## Eckerd College St. Petersburg 26-29 August 2004

We, members of five religious traditions – Buddhism, Christianity, Hinduism, Islam, and Judaism – came to think together about the responsibility of our traditions to address the problems of today, especially the growing violence in our world.

This thinking together which began in 1999 came out of our common desire for a new way of engaging in interreligious dialogue – thinking theologically in one another's presence. The first two meetings explored how to rethink core issues in our traditions in the light of religious plurality. Prompted by the increasing direct or indirect involvement of religion in various conflict situations, we discussed questions of religion and violence in the third meeting. That discussion led us to realize that religious contributions to violence are often based on negative perceptions of others.

When we perceive others to be strangers, enemies, or demons, violence is likely. This recognition led us to examine how we construct and represent others. Our discussion resulted in the following conclusions.

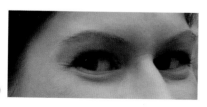
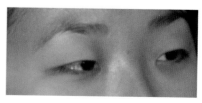

56

1. The self and others are not independent variables. Rather, self and others are interdependent; they arise together.
2. The relationship between self and others is context-dependent, ever-changing, and conditioned by power relationships.
3. We must be mindful of the dangers of abstract and static understandings of self and others. Identity is always multi-faceted, composed of many elements including gender, religion, culture, and nationality. Too often we focus on only one of our identities.
4. It is important to bring into awareness hidden and unconscious implications of our worldviews and identities that affect our relationships with others.
5. Defining self in relation to others and others in relation to self is a necessary human process. The particular identities which develop through belonging to families, communities, faith traditions, etc., can nourish a moral and compassionate human being.
6. Those whom we call "the others" are often our own projections and constructions. These constructions may be different from the way in which others represent themselves. It is important to respect the right of others to self-definition.
7. To affirm the full dignity of others, empathetic understanding and acceptance of their self-representations, though difficult, is necessary.
8. Such empathetic understanding becomes a mirror for deeper self-understanding. Through thinking together we understand **ourselves** better.
9. This process of thinking together creates mutual trust so that mutual contrition and critique are possible and safe. In such an environment we can support and challenge one another, allowing us to work together more effectively.

As religious people we must explore how our religions contribute to negative as well as positive representations

of others, and re-discover resources within our own traditions that enable us to overcome problems of alienation, constructions of others as enemies, and inter-communal violence. We are invited to re-discover ancient texts, stories, and symbols that build positive relationships with others. We must identify and develop reading materials, case studies, and interreligious projects that can assist us in fostering more positive relationships between ourselves and others. We must also search for new ways of interpreting our traditions and honor those who engage in such reinterpretation in our time.

The following questions may help us:

✱ How have our traditions dealt with self and others in the past? What are the present implications of this legacy?

✱ How are our traditions dealing with questions of self and others now?

✱ Who is the contemporary other for my religious community? Why do we perceive them as "others?"

✱ How do we teach people within our traditions to deal with others in positive ways?

✱ Across traditions, how can we help and support each other?

✱ How do we empower people to interpret and take responsibility for their traditions?

✱ Can we lift up living examples of interreligious cooperation not only in times of violence but also in times of peace?

✱ How can we educate our communities toward an appreciation of religious diversity that deepens appreciation of our own traditions as well?

✱ How can we build an alliance of concerned people, nurtured by the common market place of ideas?

Our world presents us with stark alternatives. Either we seek to understand each other better or we contribute to increasing violence in its many forms. Our process of thinking together has given us tools, inspiration, and hope that we can overcome violence through peaceful religious encounter. We have so much to gain from thinking together.

# AUTHORS

Rita M. Gross is a Buddhist scholar-practitioner who has written on issues of religion and gender and on inter-religious issues. Her Ph. D. in the History of Religions is from the University of Chicago for the first dissertation on the feminist study of religion and she is a senior teacher in one of the lineages of Tibetan Vajrayana Buddhism. Her best known book is *Buddhism after Patriarchy: A Feminist History, Analysis, and Reconstruction of Buddhism*, which has recently been translated into Spanish and Korean.

Rabia Terri Harris is founder and coordinator of the Muslim Peace Fellowship, an influential forum for progressive Muslim thought. In this role she writes and speaks widely on a variety of Islamic issues. Harris also serves as associate editor of Fellowship magazine, the bimonthly publication of the Fellowship of Reconciliation, the oldest, largest, interfaith, international peace and justice organization in the world. A scholar of Islamic studies and translator of medieval Arabic mystical texts, Harris is a senior member of the Jerrahi Order, a three-hundred-year-old Muslim religious sodality headquartered in Istanbul. Harris also practices as a chaplain attending families of children with life-threatening illnesses, regardless of religion, through Valley Home Care, Valley Hospital, Ridgewood, New Jersey, USA.

A. Rashied Omar is Coordinator of the Kroc Institute's Program in Religion, Conflict and Peacebuilding (PRCP), University of Notre Dame. He is as an Imam from South Africa and author of *Tolerance, Civil Society and Renaissance: A South African Muslim Perspective* (Cape Town: Claremont Main

Road Mosque, 2002). He earned his Ph.D in religious studies from the University of Cape Town in 2005.

The Revd. Dr. M. Thomas Thangaraj is an ordained Presbyter of the Church of South India and served on the faculty of Tamilnadu Theological Seminary, Madurai, India. Currently he occupies the D. W. and Ruth Brooks Chair on World Christianity at Candler School of Theology, Emory University, Atlanta, GA, U. S. A. and splits his time between teaching at Emory during spring, and directing the Bishop Stephen Neill Study and Research Centre at Palayankottai, Tamilnadu, India, during autumn. His publications include *The Crucified Guru: An Experiment in Cross-Cultural Christology* (Abingdon, 1994), *Relating to People of Other Religions: What Every Christian Needs to Know* (Abingdon, 1997) and *The Common Task: A Theology of Christian Mission* (Abingdon, 1999).

Anantanand Rambachan is Professor of Religion and Philosophy at Saint Olaf College in Minnesota. He is the author of several books, book-chapters and articles in scholarly journals. His books include, *The Limits of Scripture, Accomplishing the Accomplished*, and *"The Advaita Worldview: God, World and Humanity."*

The Rev. Dr. Hans Ucko was born in Sweden and earned his doctorate in theology at the Senate of Serampore College, Calcutta, India. Since 1989 he is the Program Executive for the Office of Interreligious Relations and Dialogue of the World Council of Churches (WCC). His publications include *The People and the People of God - Minjung and Dalit Theology in Interaction with Jewish-Christian Dialogue*, Munster: LIT-Verlag, 2002 and *Common Roots – New Horizons - Learning about Christian Faith from Dialogue with Jews*, Geneva, WCC, 1994.

Dr. Deborah Weissman, a native of the US, has resided in Jerusalem since 1972. She is a Jewish educator, currently on the faculty of the Mandel Leadership Institute. Since the mid-1980's, she has been involved in interfaith teaching and dialogue, both locally and internationally. Her specific interests include teacher training, feminism and the religious peace movement.